the BIG BOOK of MAGIC COFFEE HAIR cartoons

by

JIM SHOENBILL

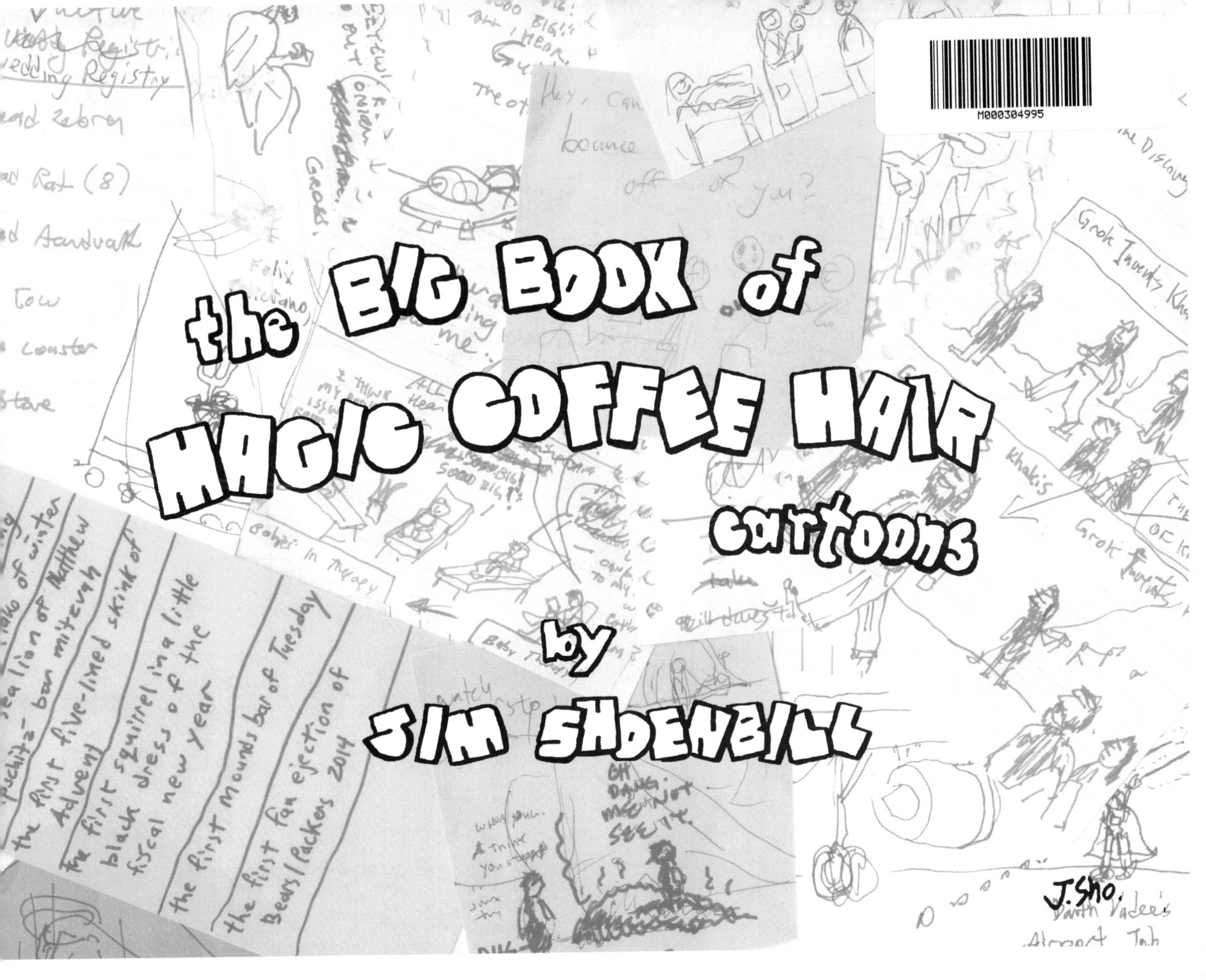
the first five-lined skink of Advent
the first squirrel in a little black dress of the fiscal new year
the first Mounds bar of Tuesday
the first fan ejection of Bears/Packers 2014
Grok Invents Khakis
Babies in Therapy
J.Sho.
Darth Vader's Airport Job

ISBN: 978-0-578-42393-7

For more Magic Coffee Hair please visit: magiccoffeehair.com
or email Jim at:
magiccoffeehair@gmail.com

<u>Other Magic Coffee Hair Collections</u>
It's a Magic Coffee Hair Life
The Magic Coffee Hair Boys and the Secret of the Smiling Monkey
Too Much Zucchini: Magic Coffee Hair Holiday Recipes

DOES THIS SMELL NORMAL TO YOU?

Magic Coffee Hair and Parenting

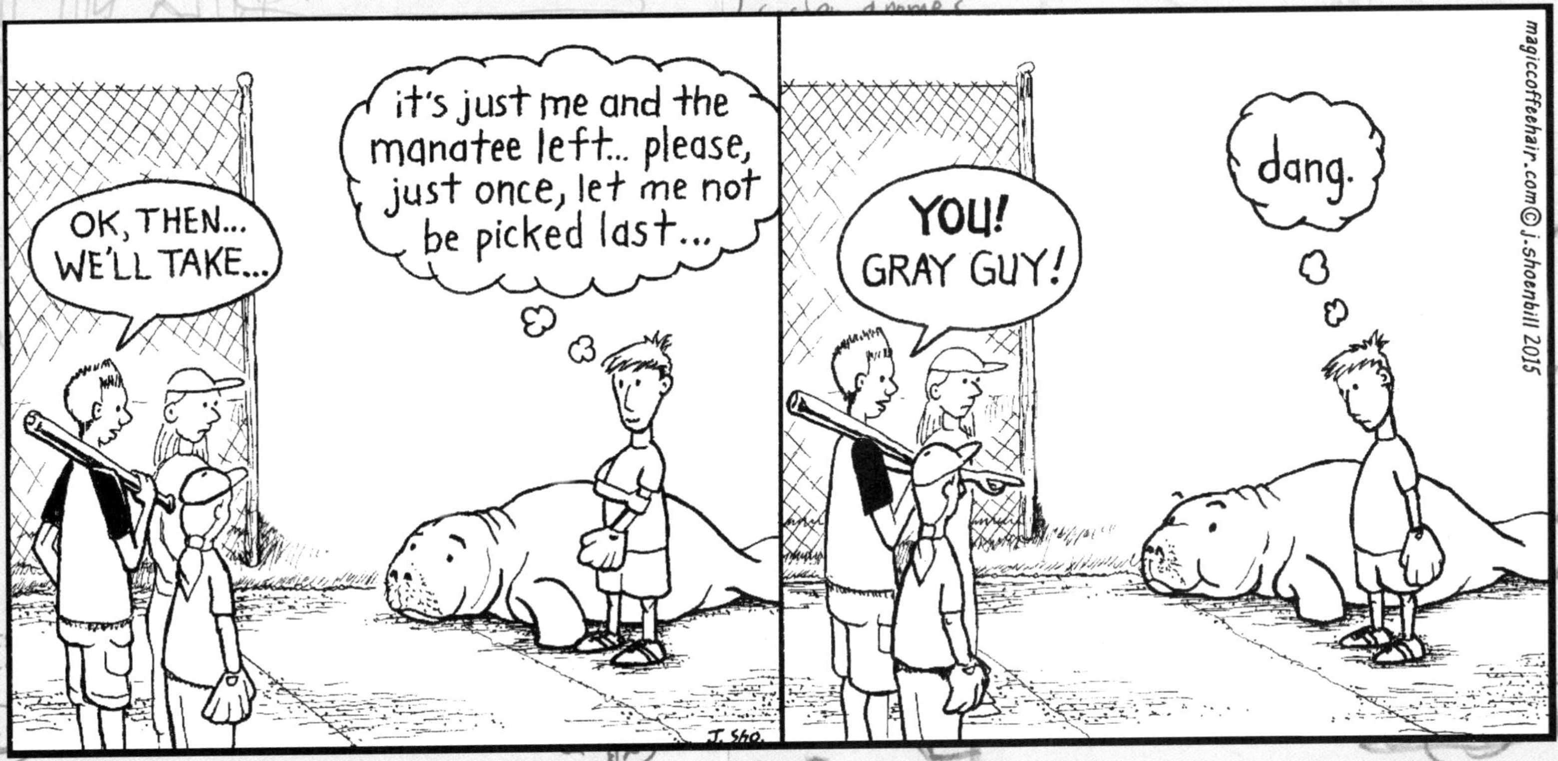

OK, THEN... WE'LL TAKE...
it's just me and the manatee left... please, just once, let me not be picked last...
J. Sho.
YOU! GRAY GUY!
dang.
magiccoffeehair.com©j.shoenbill 2015

Magic Coffee Hair and Parenting

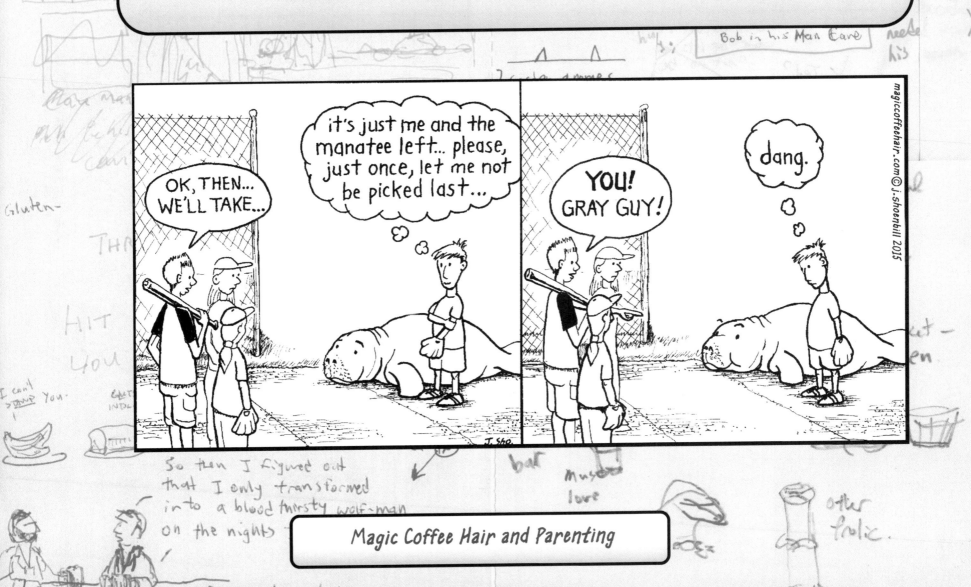

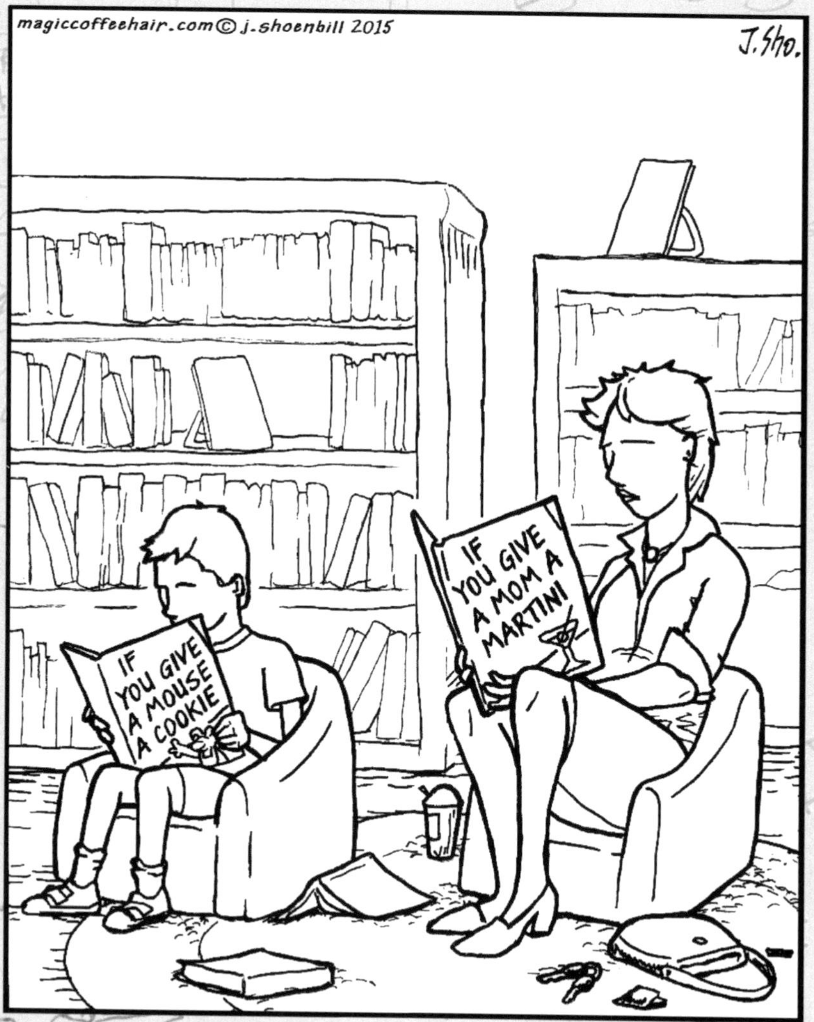
magiccoffeehair.com © j.shoenbill 2015
J.Sho.
IF YOU GIVE A MOUSE A COOKIE
IF YOU GIVE A MOM A MARTINI

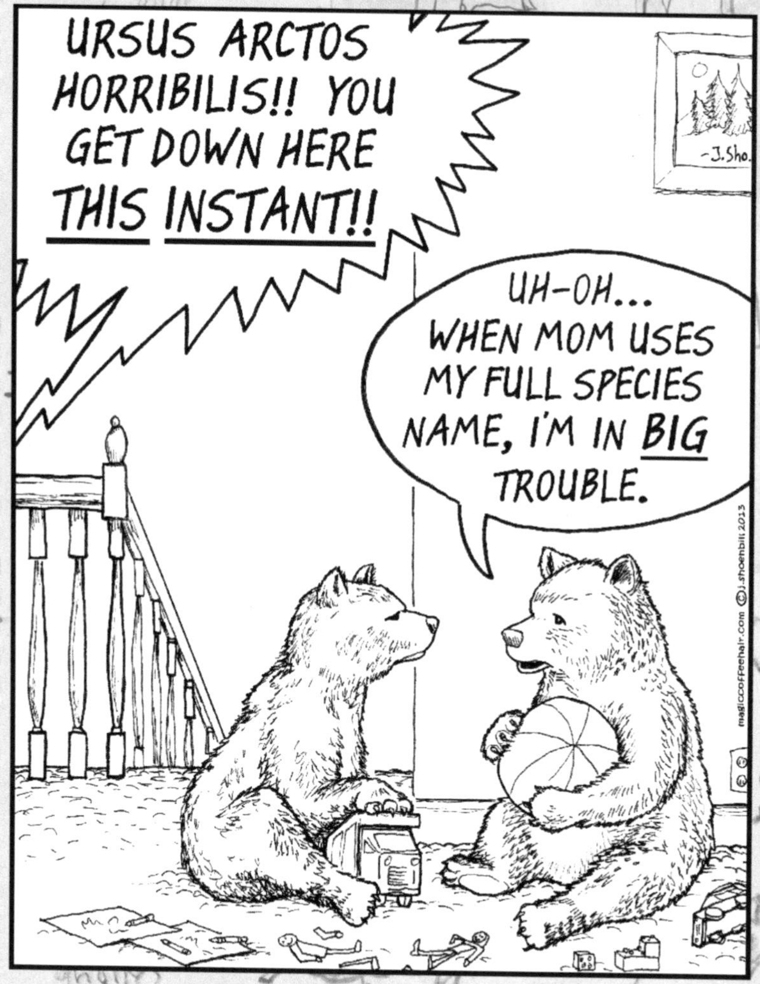
URSUS ARCTOS HORRIBILIS!! YOU GET DOWN HERE THIS INSTANT!!
UH-OH... WHEN MOM USES MY FULL SPECIES NAME, I'M IN BIG TROUBLE.
-J.Sho.
magiccoffeehair.com © j.shoenbill 2013

Magic Coffee Hair and Parenting

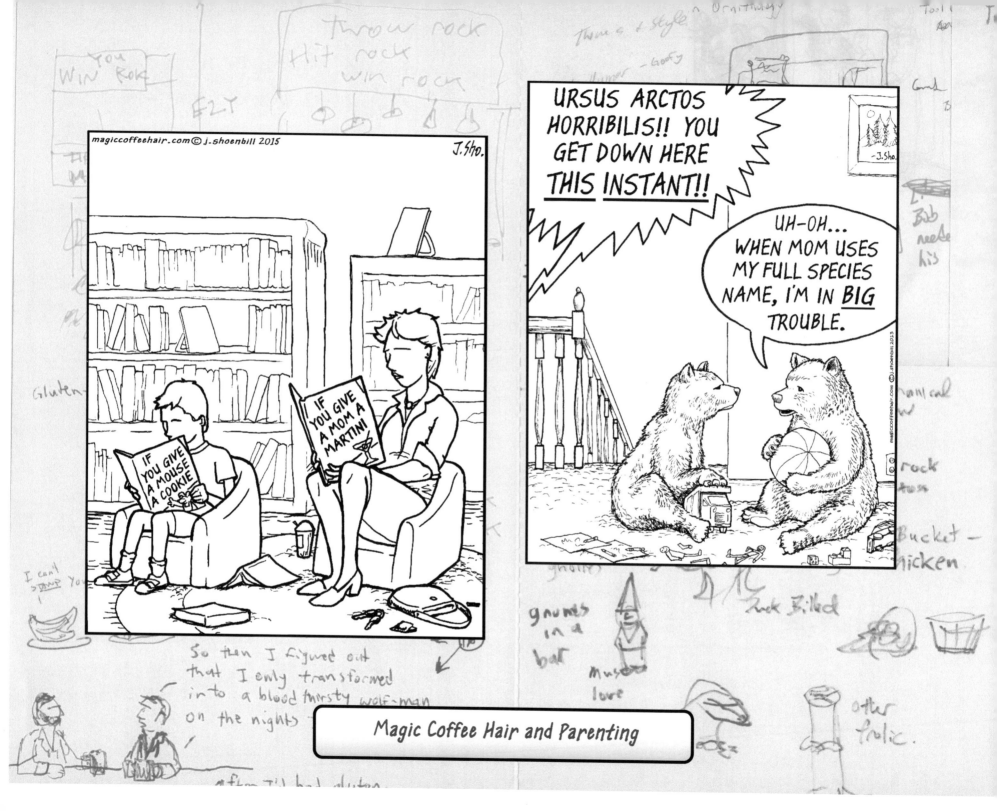

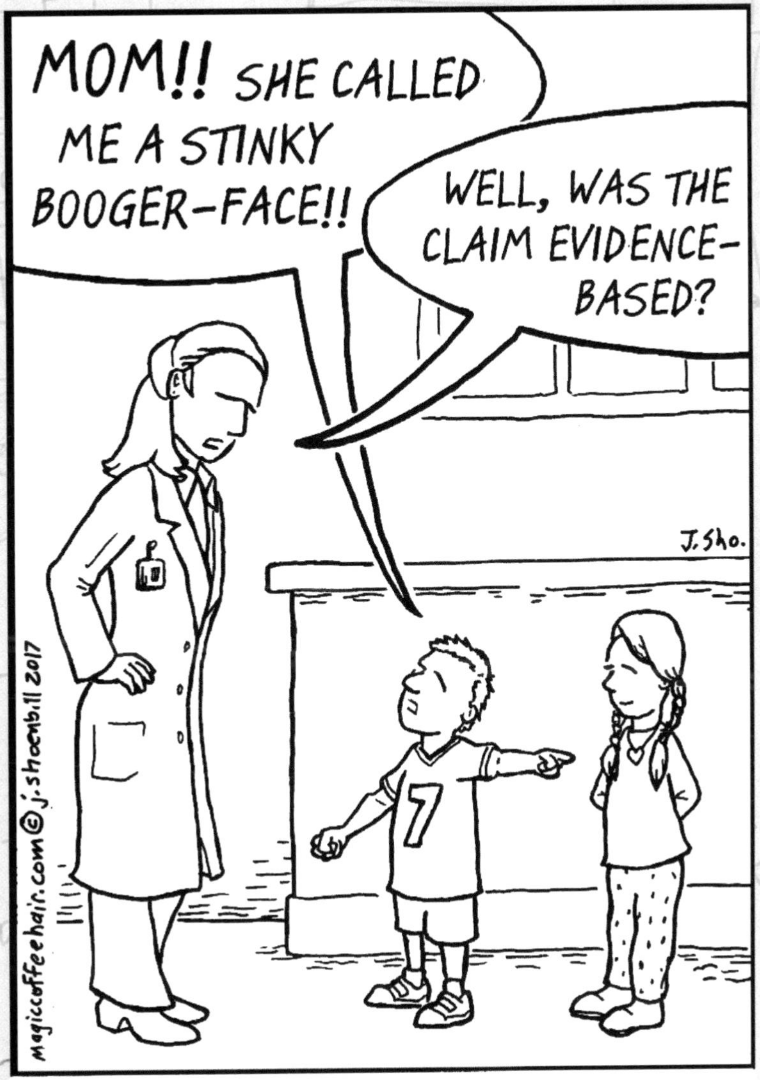

MOM!! SHE CALLED ME A STINKY BOOGER-FACE!!
WELL, WAS THE CLAIM EVIDENCE-BASED?
J.Sho.
magiccoffeehair.com © j.shoenbill 2017

Scientist Parents

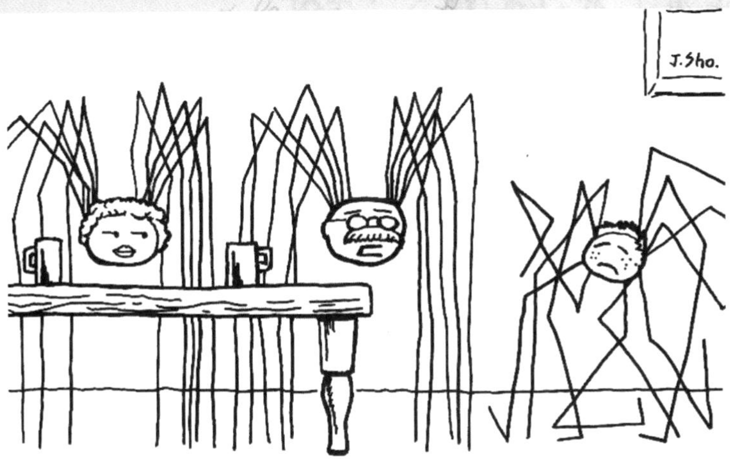

J.Sho.

"Don't worry, son. You're just at that awkward age."

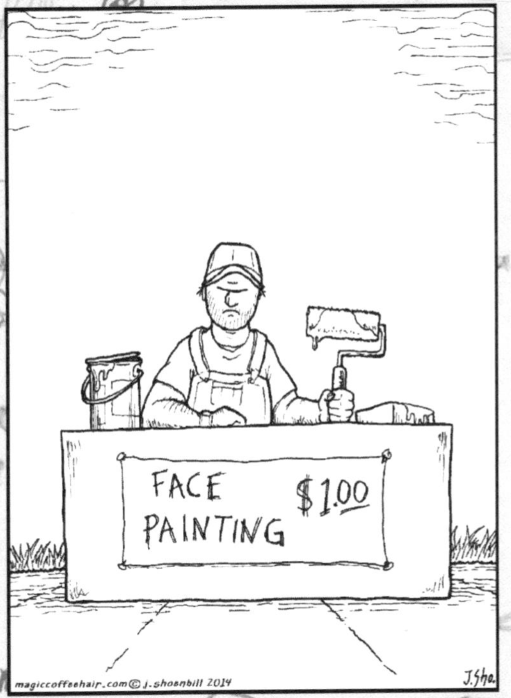

FACE PAINTING $1.00
magiccoffeehair.com © j.shoenbill 2014
J.Sho.

Magic Coffee Hair and Parenting

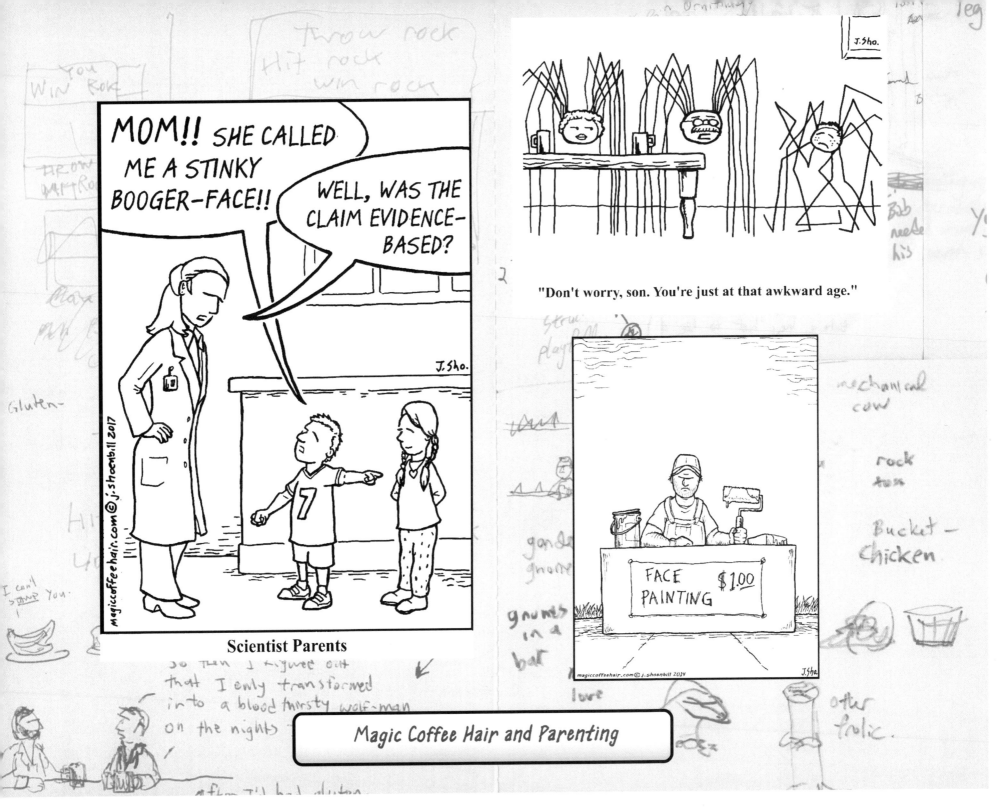

Magic Coffee Hair and Parenting

"Just once, I'd like to have a *nice* meal
in the dining room."

Einstein, to his teenagers

Magic Coffee Hair and Parenting

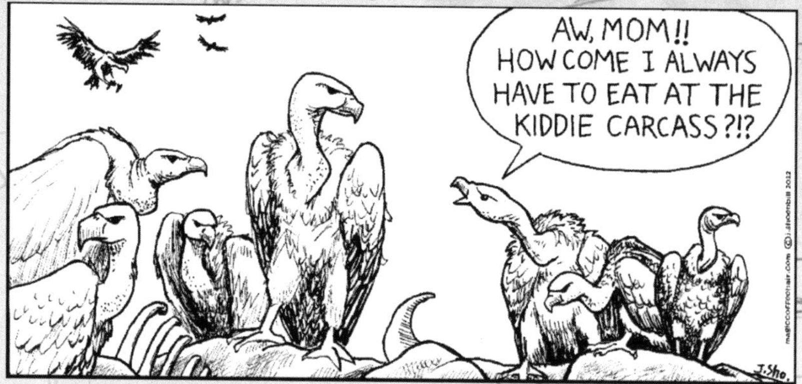
AW, MOM!!
HOW COME I ALWAYS HAVE TO EAT AT THE KIDDIE CARCASS?!?
J.Sho.

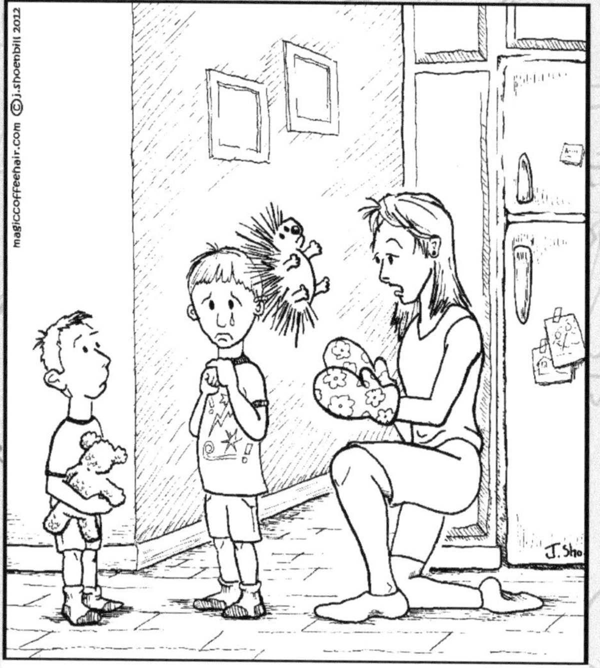
magiccoffeehair.com ©j.shoenbill 2012
J.Sho.

"Well, maybe next time you'll *listen* when Mommy tells you not to run with a porcupine."

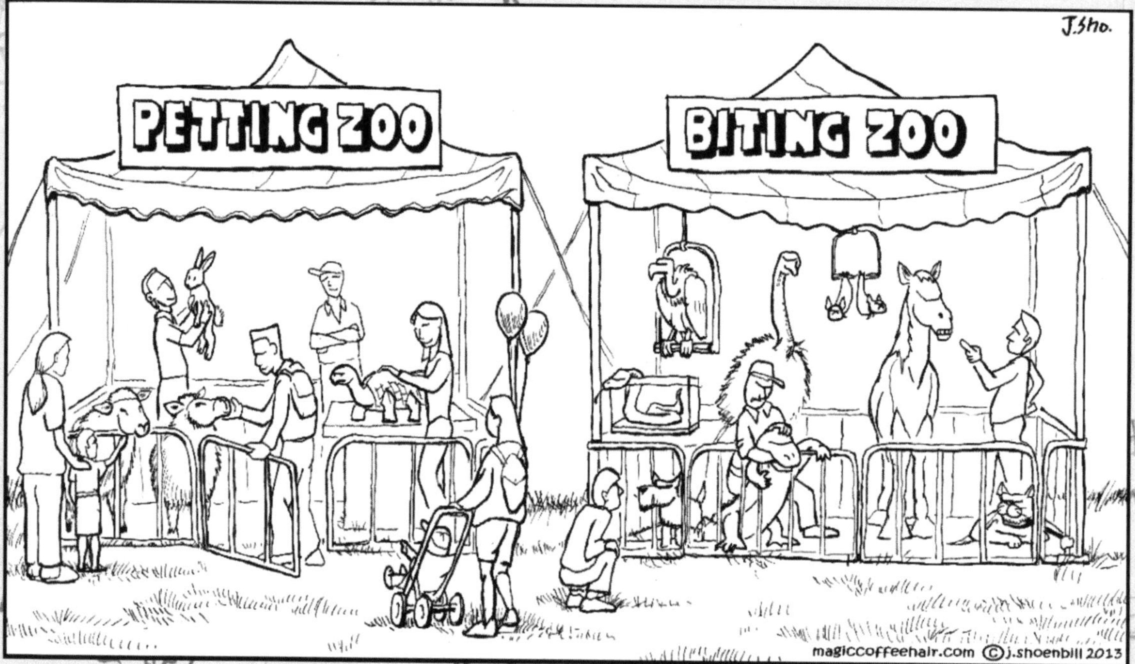
J.Sho.
PETTING ZOO
BITING ZOO
magiccoffeehair.com ©j.shoenbill 2013

Magic Coffee Hair and Parenting

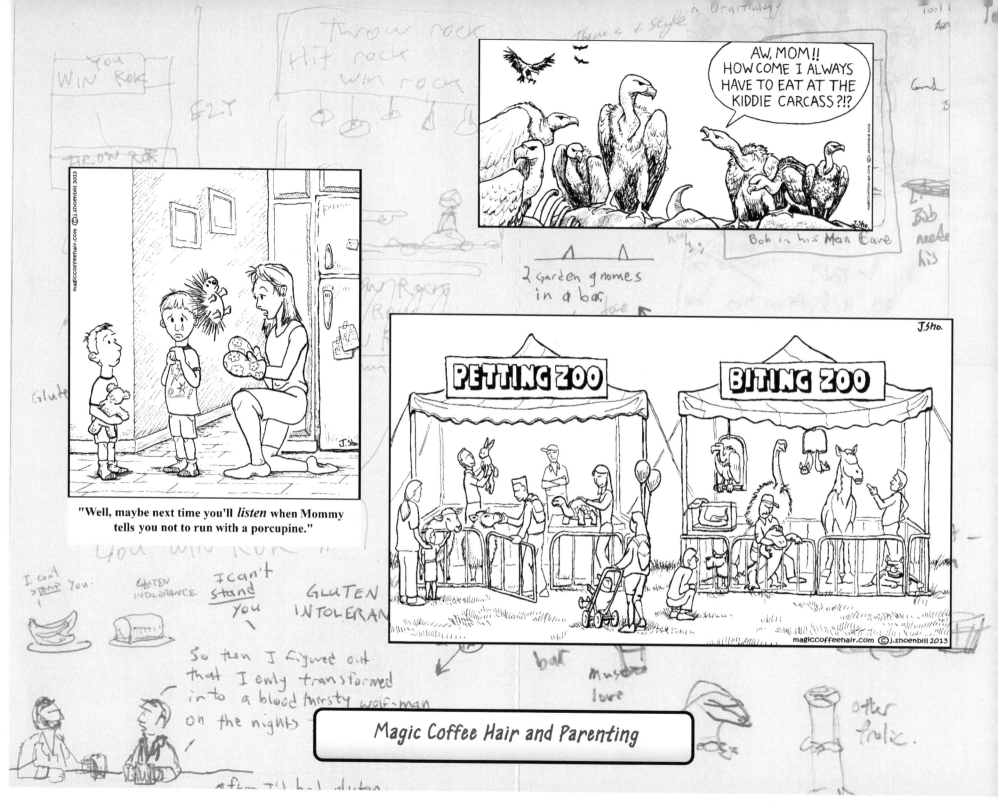

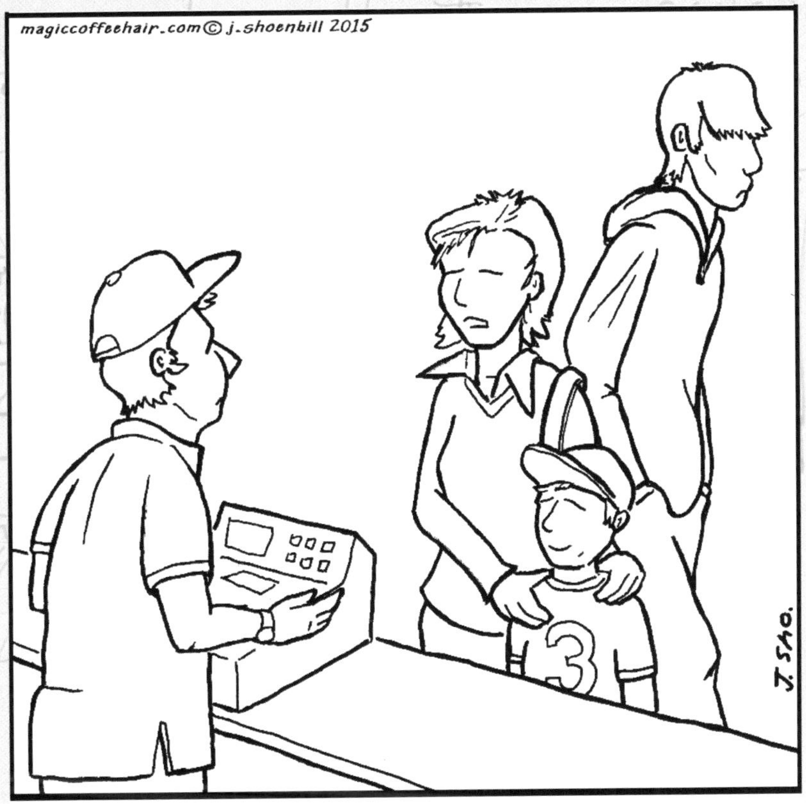
magiccoffeehair.com© j.shoenbill 2015
J. Sho.

"My six-year-old will have a Happy Meal,
my teenager will have a Sullen And Resentful Meal,
and I'll have the Oh My God Is This All There Is Meal."

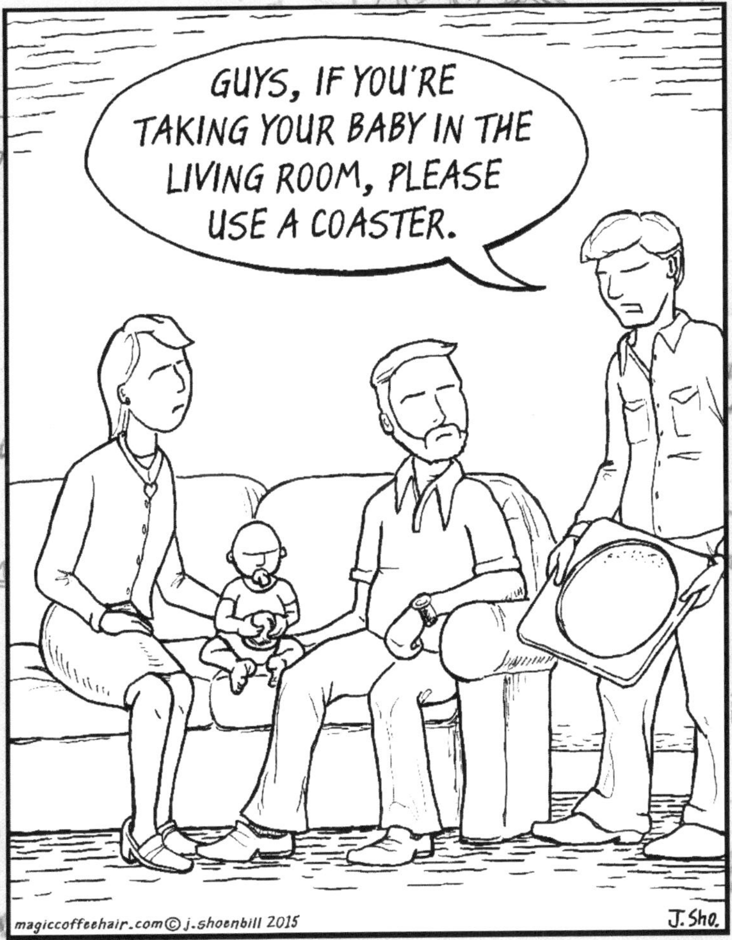
GUYS, IF YOU'RE TAKING YOUR BABY IN THE LIVING ROOM, PLEASE USE A COASTER.
magiccoffeehair.com© j.shoenbill 2015
J. Sho.

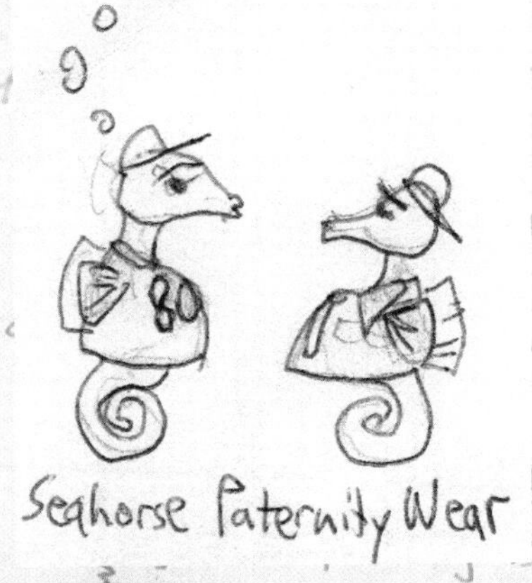
Seahorse Paternity Wear

Magic Coffee Hair and Parenting

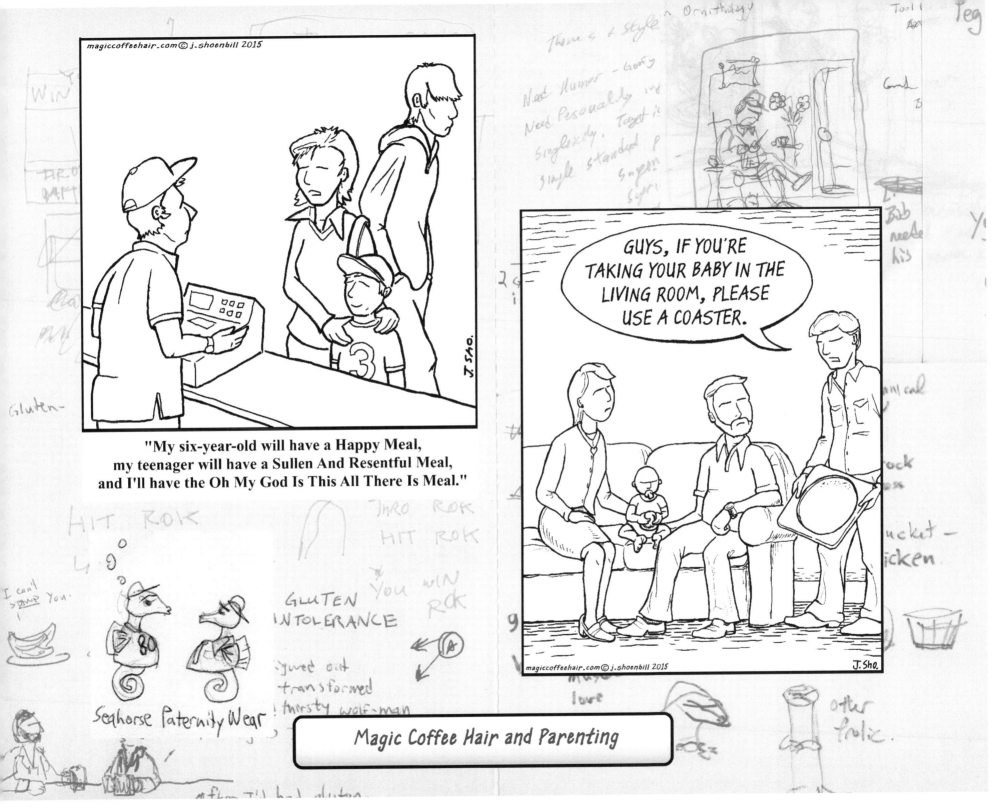

Magic Coffee Hair and Parenting

Snake teens

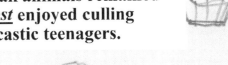

While old, sick, and weak animals remained targets, the lions *most* enjoyed culling the herd of its sarcastic teenagers.

Magic Coffee Hair and Parenting

"It's funny.. back when I first signed up to 'Adopt an Endangered Manatee', I thought they just wanted me to send money."

"Get down here and start your homework, you two. That's enough screen time for today."

Magic Coffee Hair and Parenting

Niche Extracurriculars

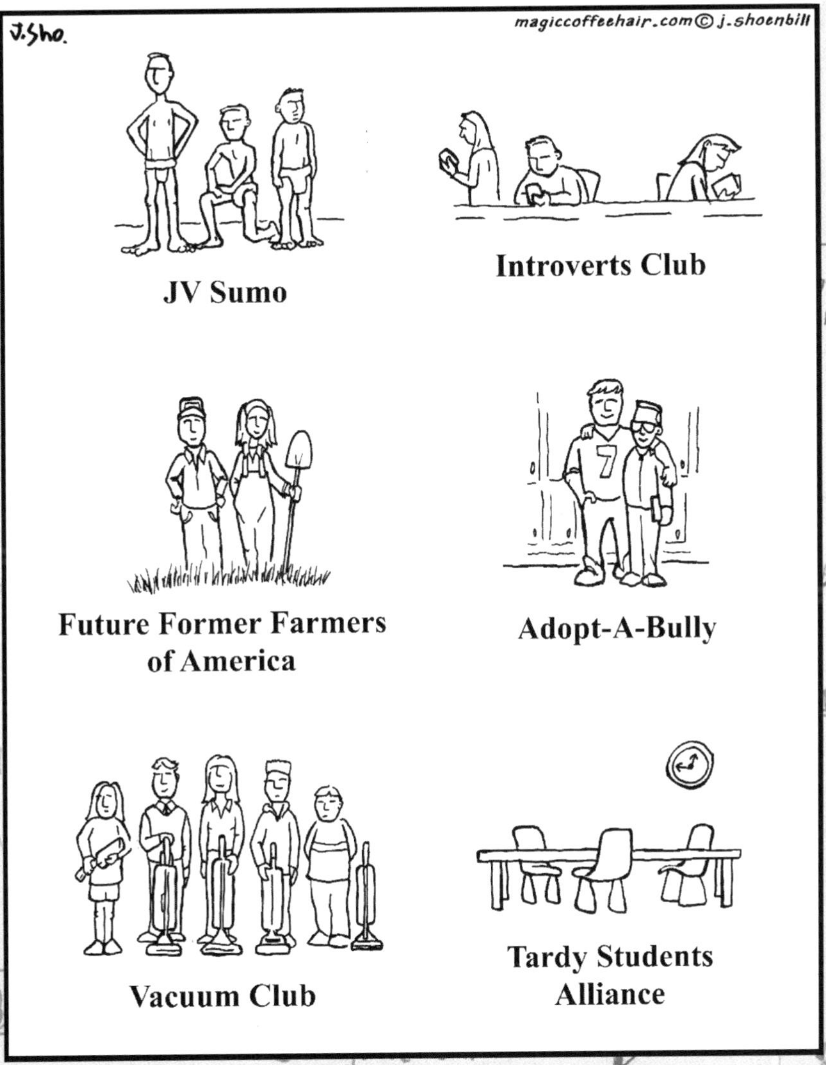
J.Sho.
magiccoffeehair.com© j.shoenbill
JV Sumo
Introverts Club
Future Former Farmers of America
Adopt-A-Bully
Vacuum Club
Tardy Students Alliance

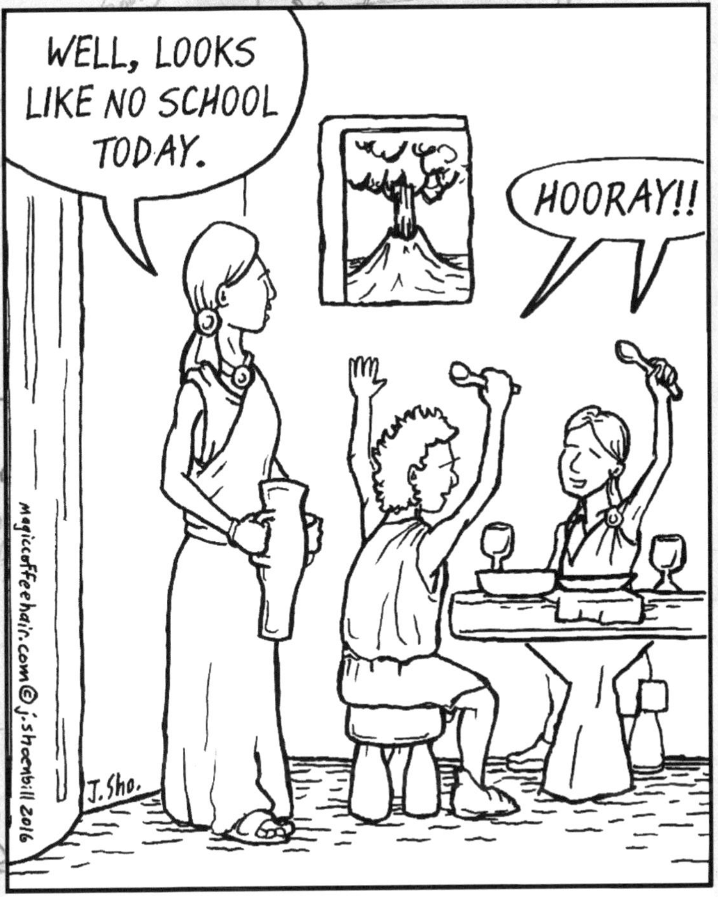
WELL, LOOKS LIKE NO SCHOOL TODAY.
HOORAY!!
magiccoffeehair.com© j.shoenbill 2016
J.Sho.

Pompeii kids

Magic Coffee Hair and Parenting

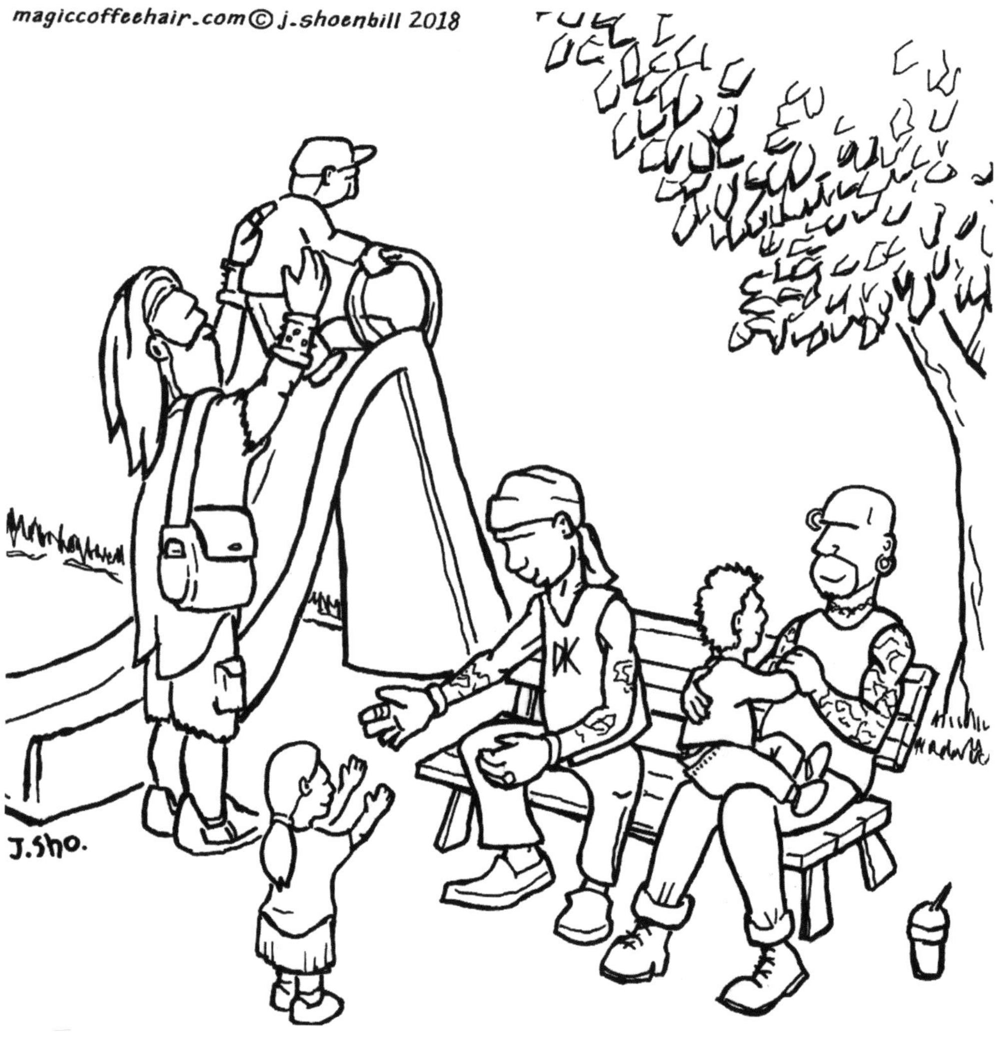
magiccoffeehair.com © j.shoenbill 2018
J.Sho.

Another pleasant morning with the South Milwaukee underground thrash-metal bassist stay-at-home dads of toddlers playgroup

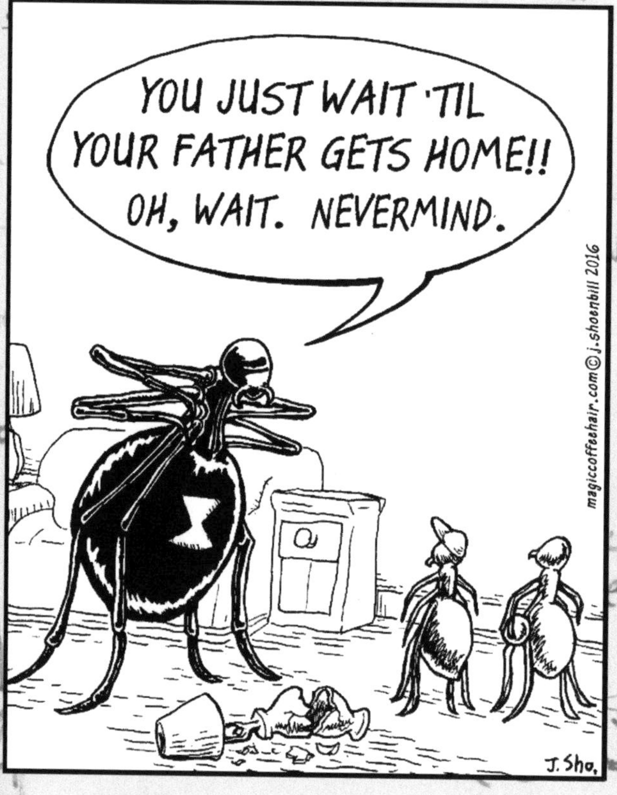
YOU JUST WAIT 'TIL YOUR FATHER GETS HOME!! OH, WAIT. NEVERMIND.
magiccoffeehair.com © j.shoenbill 2016
J.Sho.

Magic Coffee Hair and Parenting

CHRISTMAS 1985

Magic Coffee Hair for the Holidays

Halloween: A great excuse to clean out your junk drawer.

"My client greatly regrets the incident with the carving knife. However, in her defense, **14** people were coming for Thanksgiving and her husband, who I may remind the court had *just one job to do,* bought only **8** rolls."

Magic Coffee Hair for the Holidays

The scourge of "coffin head"

Fitted Sheet Ghosts aren't scary

YOU WILL BE VISITED BY THREE MORE GHOSTS THIS NIGHT....

Magic Coffee Hair for the Holidays

Not a Creature was Stirring

Ebenezer Scrooge is visited by the Ghost of Christmas 1985

Magic Coffee Hair for the Holidays

Magic Coffee Hair for the Holidays

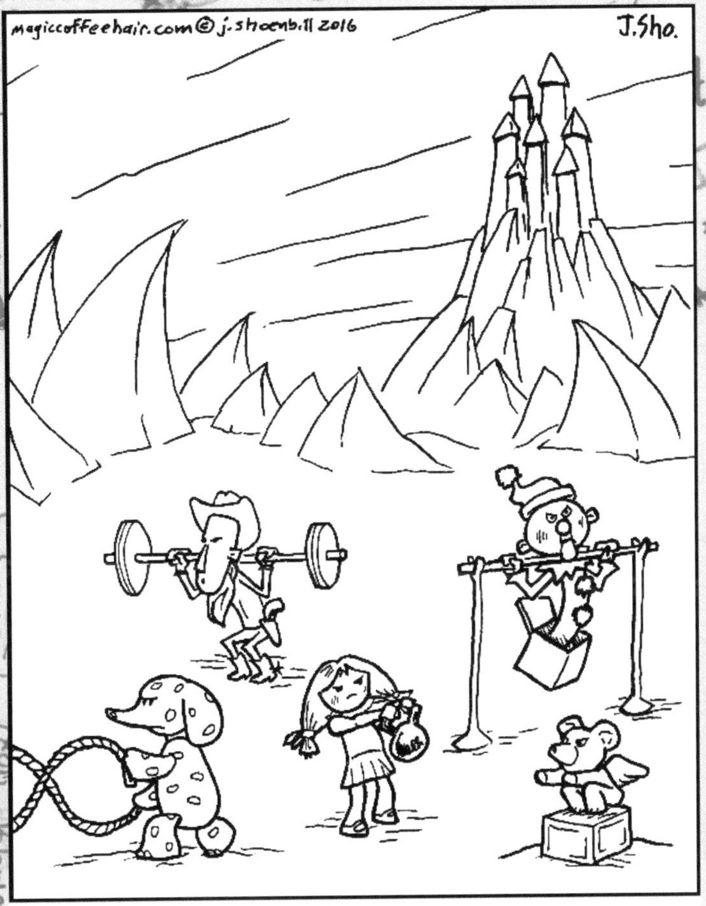
magiccoffeehair.com © j.shoenbill 2016
J.Sho.

The Island of CrossFit Toys

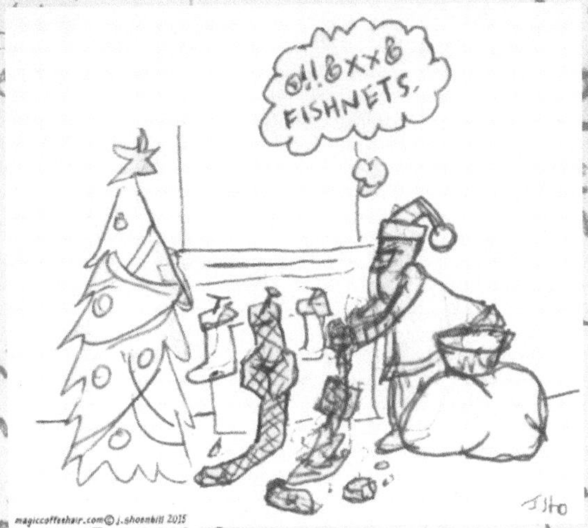
FISHNETS.
magiccoffeehair.com © j.shoenbill 2015
J.Sho

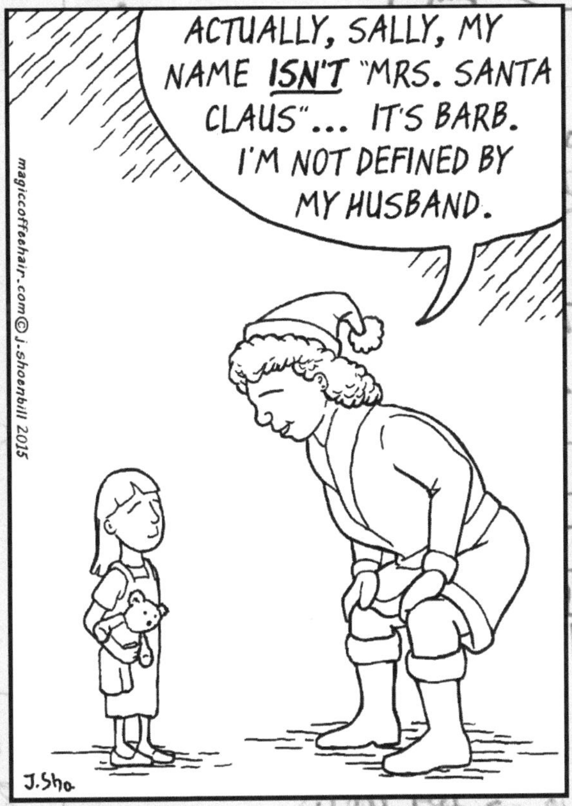
ACTUALLY, SALLY, MY NAME ISN'T "MRS. SANTA CLAUS"... IT'S BARB. I'M NOT DEFINED BY MY HUSBAND.
magiccoffeehair.com © j.shoenbill 2015
J.Sho.

Magic Coffee Hair for the Holidays

Erma's had enough of people walking off with her best Tupperware every Thanksgiving.

Magic Coffee Hair for the Holidays

OPPORTUNITIES FOR IMPROVEMENT

Magic Coffee Hair in the Workplace

"I don't want to take this meeting off track, but.. isn't *Stonehenge* amazing? Seriously, who *did* that?"

Magic Coffee Hair in the Workplace

"Tell Barb I can't make her 10:30. I have a conflict."

Ambush Predators

Stonefish

Trapdoor Spider

Vine Snake

Art Jennings, Project Manager

Carl Tipping

Magic Coffee Hair in the Workplace

Magic Coffee Hair in the Workplace

Magic Coffee Hair in the Workplace

"I *hate* these Management 'all-hands' meetings."

Project Managers in Hell

Magic Coffee Hair in the Workplace

Project Manager Showdown

Magic Coffee Hair in the Workplace

Rex is forced to sign a letter of reprimand, for his file.

"I've observed that on several occasions, when given the opportunity to assist a struggling co-worker, you instead chose merely to 'pity the fool'."

Magic Coffee Hair in the Workplace

"The quality of your work this year has been good, but concerns have been raised about your 'sense of urgency'."

"Hi. We're here to encroach on your habitat."

Magic Coffee Hair in the Workplace

SO, HOW WAS YOUR "FIVE WHYS" ANALYSIS MEETING?

WE ONLY GOT UP TO THREE "WHYS" AND A "WHAT THE HELL".

"Next, I'll be facilitating a classic team-building exercise. It's called, 'Kill the Guy with the Ball'."

Apple-to-Orange adapter

Magic Coffee Hair in the Workplace

Magic Coffee Hair in the Workplace

THIS IS AN EXIT ROW

Magic Coffee Hair Travels the World

"Attention, please: We are now offering $100 travel vouchers to any ticketholders able to fit more than twenty jumbo marshmallows in their mouth at one time."

"We have now finished boarding of our first-class passengers, Premium Elite members, active/retired military, Business Priority customers, special needs passengers, airline credit card holders, and families with small children. That leaves one guy named Bob."

"Excuse me... I think you're in my seat."

QUALITY INN

QUANTITY INN

Magic Coffee Hair Travels the World

"Sir, this is an exit row. Can you confirm that, in case of emergency, you're comfortable being the first to get the hell out?"

Magic Coffee Hair Travels the World

Bedbug Hotel Reviews

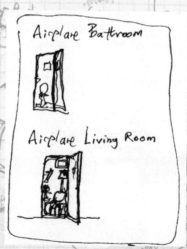

Magic Coffee Hair Travels the World

Magic Coffee Hair Travels the World

Rhonda has begun to wonder whether anyone actually listens to her safety presentations.

Magic Coffee Hair Travels the World

Bob always reads the Passenger Information Card, just to see what it says about him.

Magic Coffee Hair Travels the World

"Ladies and gentlemen, please direct your atttention to the safety presentation. It's the only way you'll know the difference between the harmless scarlet kingsnake and the deadly Eastern coral snake."

What really, *really* happened to the dinosaurs

Magic Coffee Hair Travels the World

FOUL-SMELLING SECRETIONS

Magic Coffee Hair and the Animal Kingdom

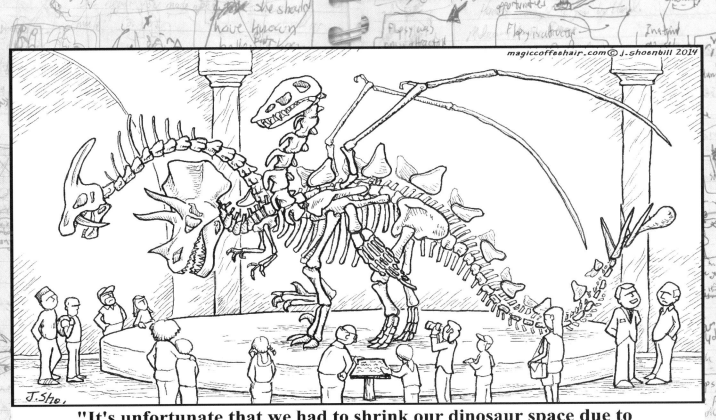

magiccoffeehair.com © j.shoenbill 2014

"It's unfortunate that we had to shrink our dinosaur space due to budget cuts. On the bright side, TriStegoApatoPlesioSaurodon Rex here is now our most popular exhibit."

Magic Coffee Hair and the Animal Kingdom

The Animal Kingdom Salutes Humanity

Mullett Lions

Natural Selection: Animal Defense Mechanisms

sparkly tiara | pointy antlers | ear-piercing shriek | sarcasm

stinging tentacles | whisk | disapproving glance | actually shoot blood from eyes

foul-smelling secretion | tiny ukulele | idle threats | threats

Magic Coffee Hair and the Animal Kingdom

Magic Coffee Hair and the Animal Kingdom

Magic Coffee Hair and the Animal Kingdom

Magic Coffee Hair and the Animal Kingdom

"Carol, is everything alright?
You don't seem sluggish today."

Compliment-A-Mole

Bob worries that his new neighbor may be bad for business.

Magic Coffee Hair and the Animal Kingdom

To Rough up a Mockingbird

Less-common frisbee animals

Frisbee cat

Frisbee snake

frisbee tortoise

frisbee squid

frisbee hermit crab

IT'S WORKING! HE'S COMING CLOSER! MAKE THE SOUND AGAIN!!

PPSHHT!!

EMPLOYEES MUST LICK THEMSELVES BEFORE RETURNING TO WORK

Magic Coffee Hair and the Animal Kingdom

Magic Coffee Hair and the Animal Kingdom

Magic Coffee Hair and the Animal Kingdom

Bob finds that from the top of a tall building, the people all look like ants.

Wildlife in leather vests. No reason.

Magic Coffee Hair and the Animal Kingdom

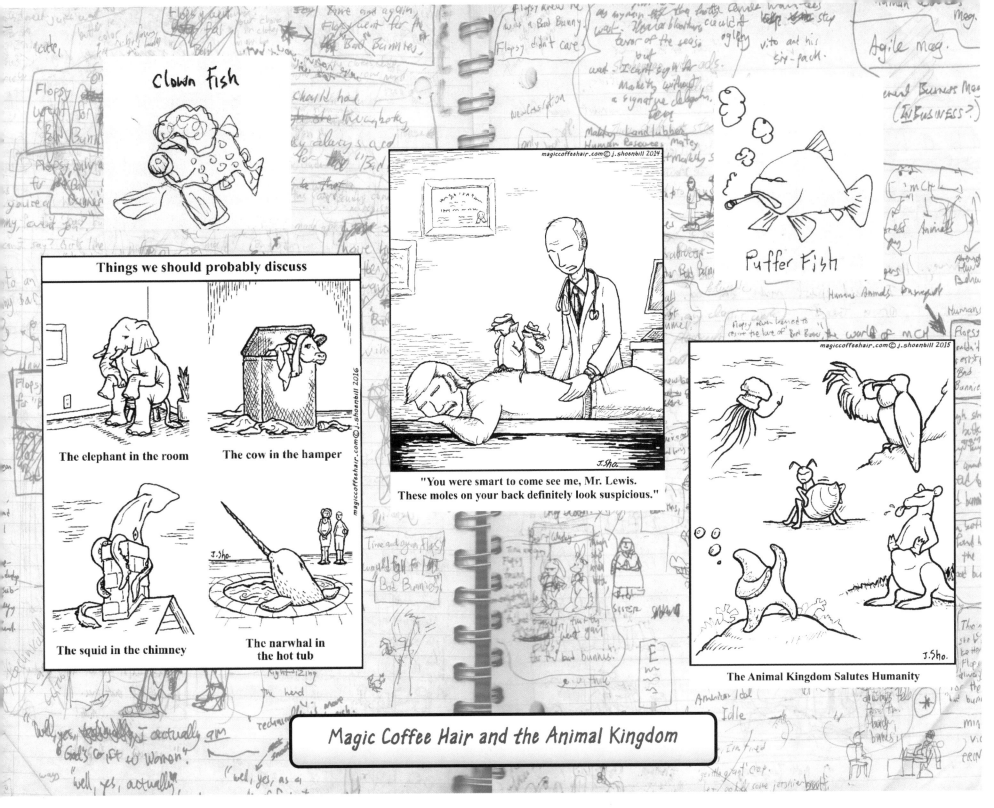

Magic Coffee Hair and the Animal Kingdom

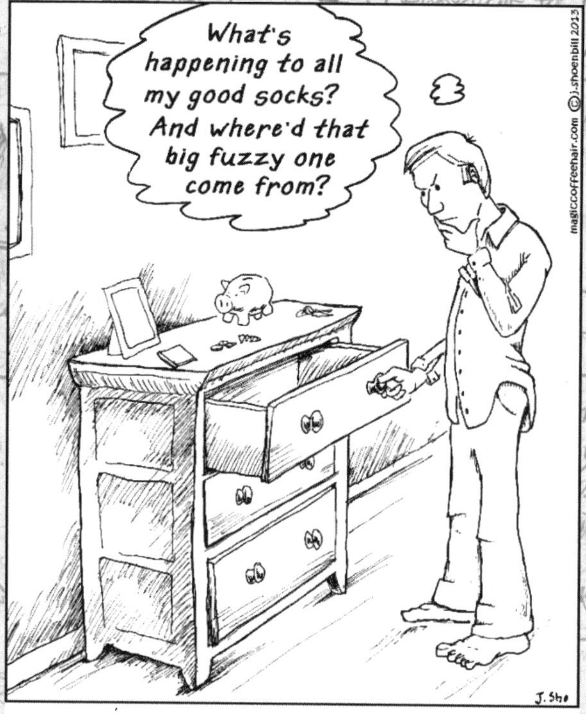
What's happening to all my good socks? And where'd that big fuzzy one come from?
magiccoffeehair.com © J.shoenbill 2013
J. Sho

Invasive species reach Ken's sock drawer.

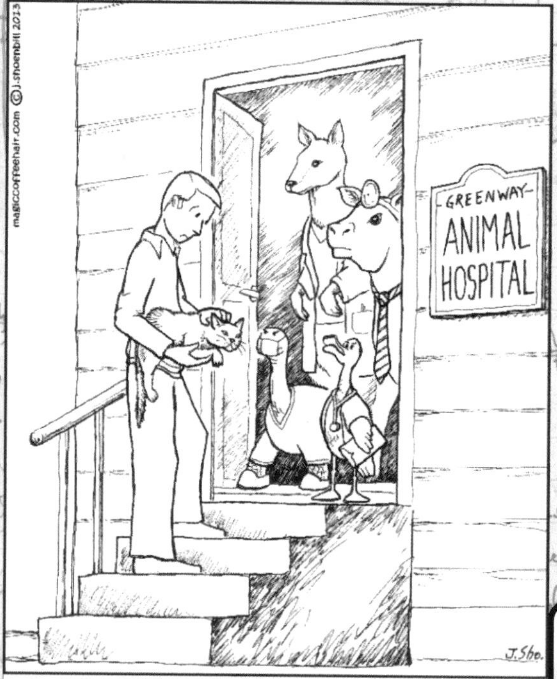
magiccoffeehair.com © J.shoenbill 2013
GREENWAY
ANIMAL HOSPITAL
J.Sho.

"Well, what were you expecting?"

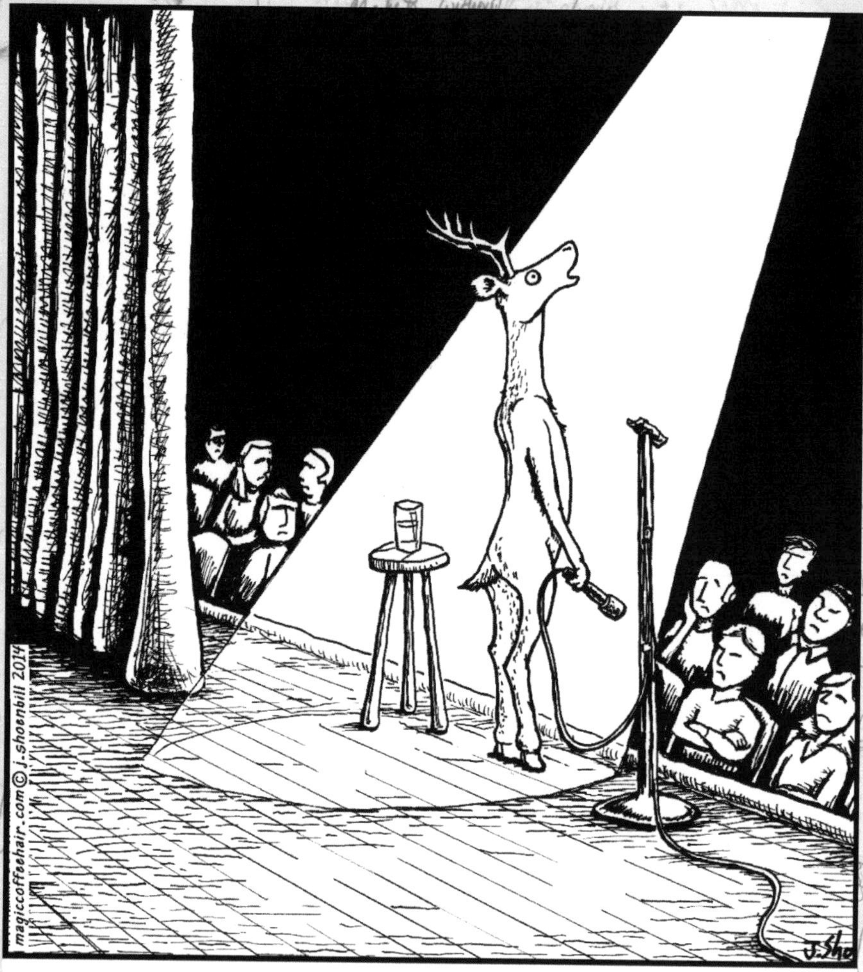
magiccoffeehair.com © J.shoenbill 2014
J.Sho

Bucky's dream of becoming a stand-up comedian ended abruptly the very first time he stepped into the spotlight.

Magic Coffee Hair and the Animal Kingdom

"No, you idiot! Use the corkscrew!!"

House Hunters

Magic Coffee Hair and the Animal Kingdom

Tool Use in Primates

Chimpanzee

Capuchin Monkey

Sumatran Orangutan

Jim

magiccoffeehair.com © j.shoenbill 2016

CAFÉ

NO: PETS SMOKING

"Looks like you're gonna have to finish that out here, Rupert."

email: magiccoffeehair@gmail.com

magiccoffeehair.com © j.shoenbill 2017

Magic Coffee Hair and the Animal Kingdom

YOU'RE BEING CLINGY

Love, Magic Coffee Hair Style

Love, Magic Coffee Hair Style

Love, Magic Coffee Hair Style

Love, Magic Coffee Hair Style

"Oh, look. Better put me down, honey."

"I believe we told you **quite** clearly not to let his stitches get wet."

Love, Magic Coffee Hair Style

Backseat predators

Try as they might, the female manatees could not keep from ogling Ivan and his "six-pack".

Love, Magic Coffee Hair Style

Love, Magic Coffee Hair Style

Dan prepares to throw rice
on the happy couple.

Love, Magic Coffee Hair Style

Love, Magic Coffee Hair Style

YOU'RE OUT, BARTHOLEMEW!!
Magic Coffee Hair for the Faithful

Magic Coffee Hair for the Faithful

The Teachings of Jesus: Day 1

"I've got to be honest. It's going to be hard to find you a position that offers 40 days of personal time."

Magic Coffee Hair for the Faithful

Pastor Andy's pet peeves finally get the better of him.

"Well, actually, yes... I _do_ think I'm God's Gift to Women."

Magic Coffee Hair for the Faithful

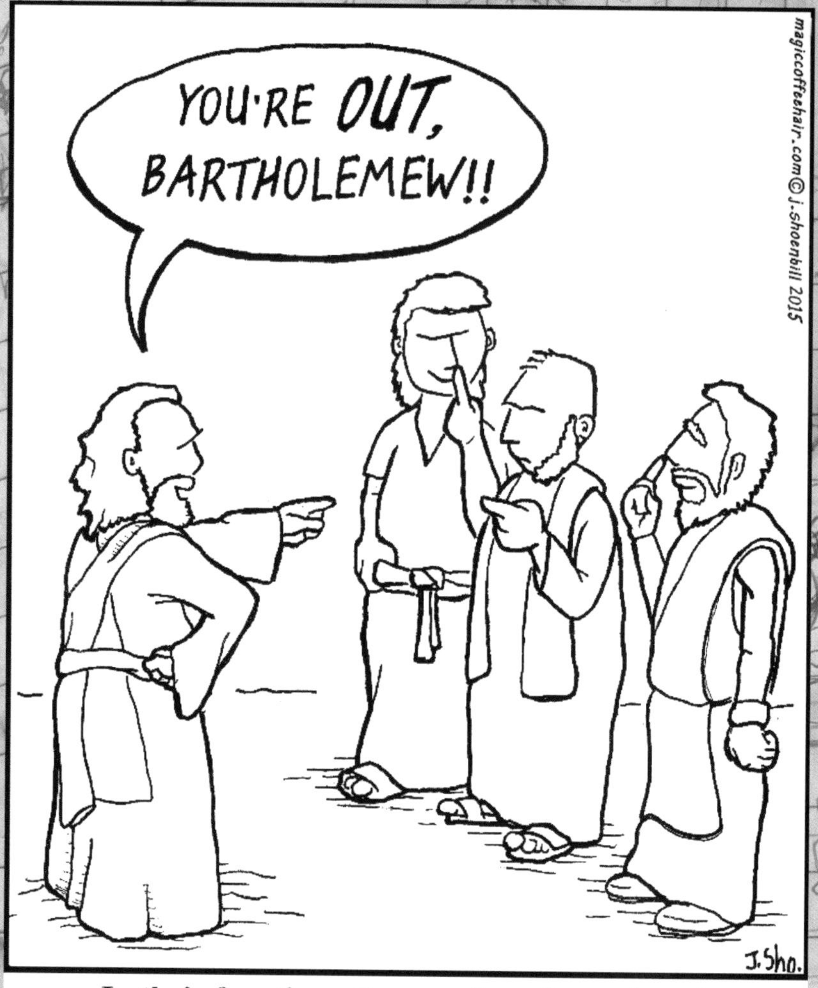
YOU'RE OUT, BARTHOLEMEW!!
magiccoffeehair.com© j.shoenbill 2015
J.Sho.

In their free time, the apostles often enjoyed rousing games of "Simon Peter Says".

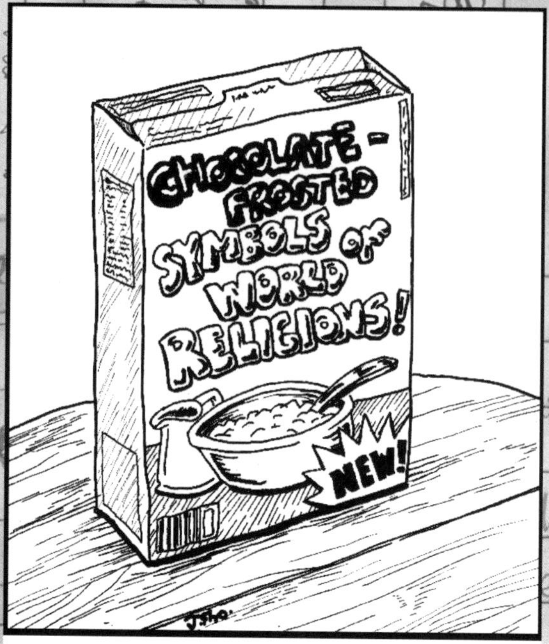
CHOCOLATE-FROSTED SYMBOLS OF WORLD RELIGIONS!
NEW!

Bad product concepts

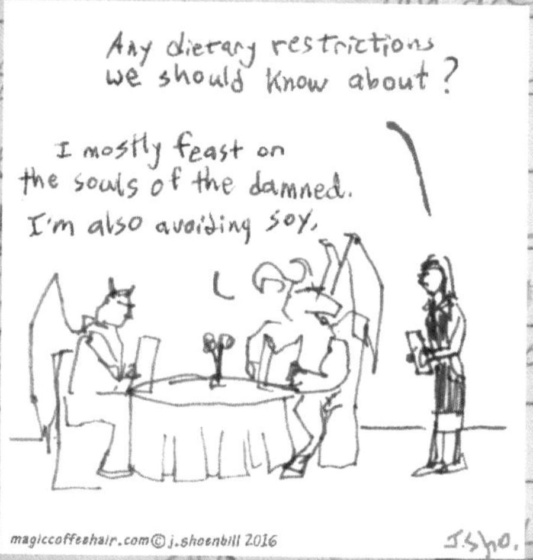
Any dietary restrictions we should know about?
I mostly feast on the souls of the damned. I'm also avoiding soy.
magiccoffeehair.com© j.shoenbill 2016
J.Sho.

Magic Coffee Hair for the Faithful

Figure 1. Lesser-known Apostles

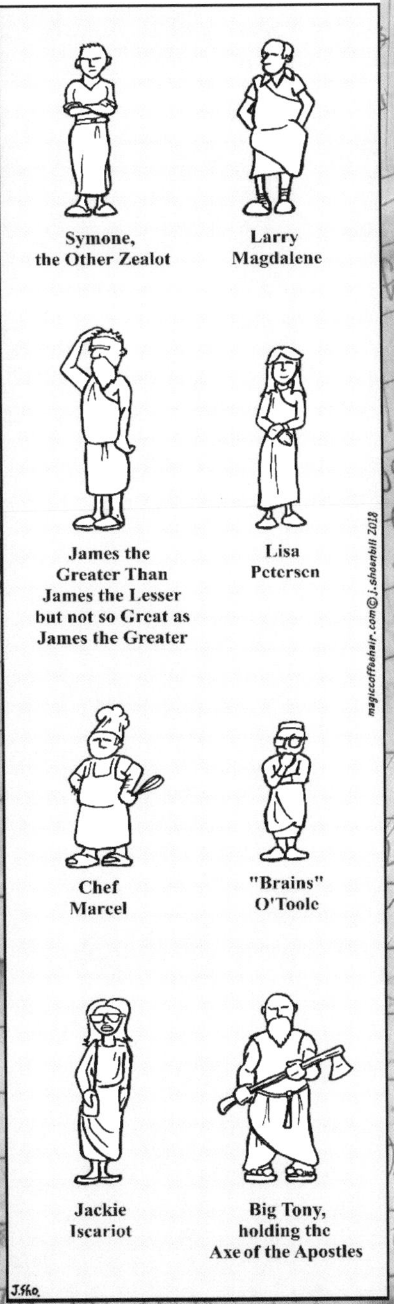
Symone,
the Other Zealot
Larry
Magdalene
James the
Greater Than
James the Lesser
but not so Great as
James the Greater
Lisa
Petersen
Chef
Marcel
"Brains"
O'Toole
Jackie
Iscariot
Big Tony,
holding the
Axe of the Apostles
magiccoffeehair.com© j.shoenbill 2018
J.Sho.

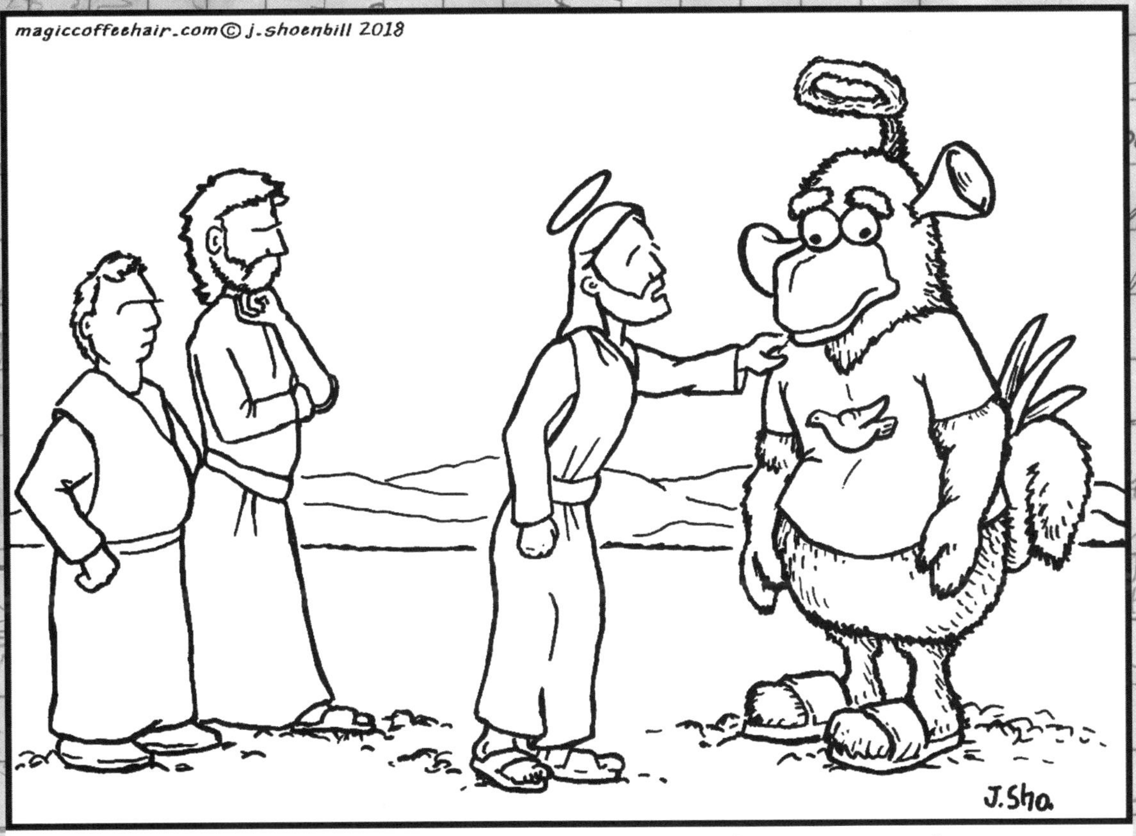
magiccoffeehair.com© j.shoenbill 2018
J.Sha

"I'm sorry Gary, but my twelve apostles are enough.
We don't also need a mascot."

Magic Coffee Hair for the Faithful

Teen Jesus

"Let me guess.. Military, right?"

Magic Coffee Hair for the Faithful

HOW TO CLEAN ALMOST ANYTHING

Magic Coffee Hair Odds and Ends

Magic Coffee Hair Odds and Ends

"Hold up, Jesse... I better pull over.
My **CHECK HORSE** light just came on."

Clowns marking their territory

Magic Coffee Hair Odds and Ends

"Dangit. We'll never get it down *now*."

"Sir, I'm afraid we can't accept this as a form of identification."

well, tell Dr. Jenkins that if I was speaking to him, I'd tell him he was being a big fat jerk.

Floaties

Sinkies

TONY

Magic Coffee Hair Odds and Ends

bagpiper fashion options

- traditional kilt
- mini-kilt
- pencil kilt
- hoop-kilt
- yoga pants

Oh, Lord... what did I make??

Binge scrapbooking: the morning after

Siege Tailgating

Native Tribe hunting using blowguns

Less-successful Native Tribe hunting using spitballs

Magic Coffee Hair Odds and Ends

Agricultural Psychology

Magic Coffee Hair Odds and Ends

Corn on the Cob

corn on the remote control

Corn on the Pizza cutter

Corn on Fred Jenkins

SHEESH... MISSED A BUTTON **AGAIN**.

Knights of the Coffee Table

Figure 1. murphies

murphy bed

murphy aquarium

murphy Twister® pad

murphy can of chili

murphy ibex

murphy Murphy

Magic Coffee Hair Odds and Ends

"I'm home, Honey! Come see what I picked up at the Farmers Market!!"

It would be weeks before Mike noticed the sign painters' unfortunate error.

Magic Coffee Hair Odds and Ends

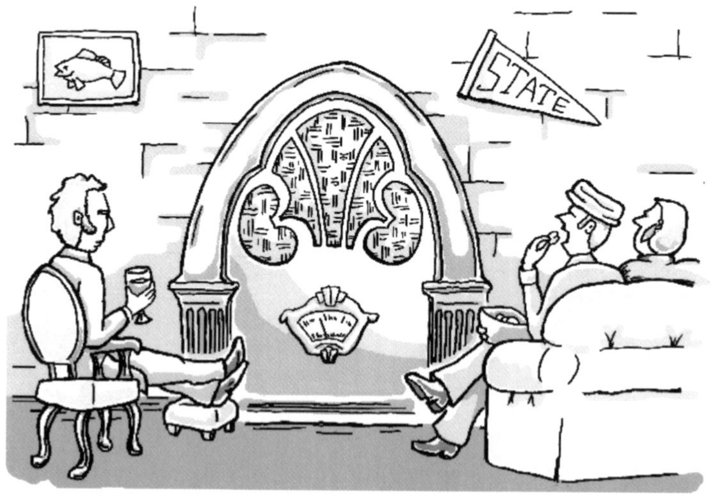
STATE

Pre-Television Man Caves

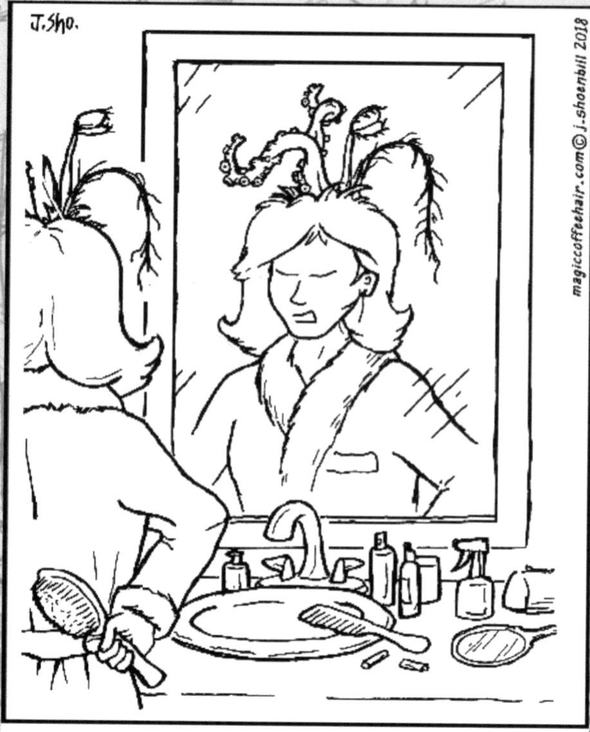
J.Sho.
magiccoffeehair.com© j.shoenbill 2018

"Ugh. I *hate* my hair."

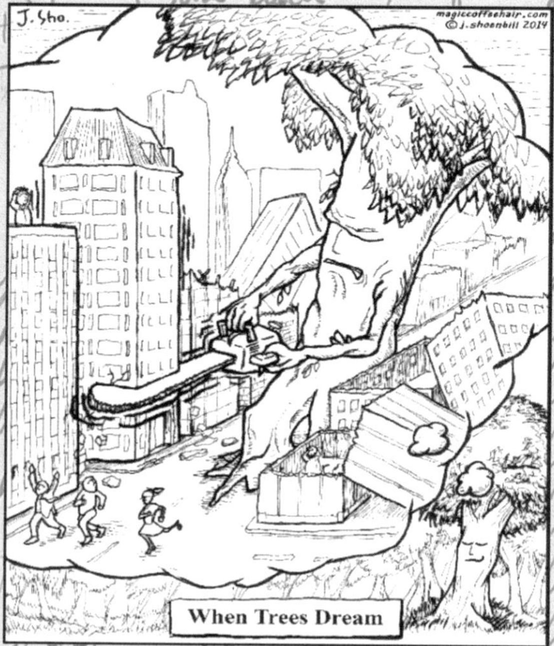
J. Sho.
magiccoffeehair.com
© j.shoenbill 2014

When Trees Dream

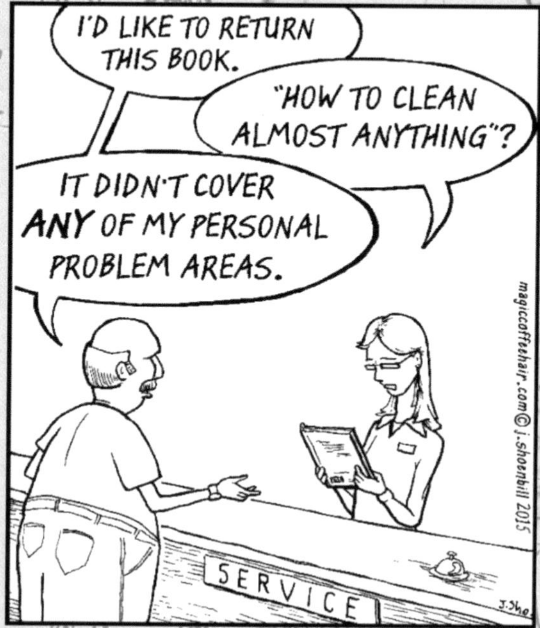
I'D LIKE TO RETURN THIS BOOK.
"HOW TO CLEAN ALMOST ANYTHING"?
IT DIDN'T COVER **ANY** OF MY PERSONAL PROBLEM AREAS.
SERVICE
magiccoffeehair.com© j.shoenbill 2015
J.Sho

Magic Coffee Hair Odds and Ends

The lesser-known, and ultimately unsuccessful,
Joe Louis and Dick Clark expedition.

Gary has a Floss with Death

Magic Coffee Hair Odds and Ends

when staffing agencies screw up

Magic Coffee Hair Odds and Ends

Magic Coffee Hair Odds and Ends

"I feel guilty about this, Nicky. We really should be composting."

at Compulsive Play-Doh Sniffers Anonymous

Magic Coffee Hair Odds and Ends

2018's Most Hotly Anticipated TV Shows

America's Got Hives

Ignoring the Kardashians

So You Think You Can
Perform Abdominal Surgery

America's Next
Top Actuary

Real Househusbands
of Sheboygan

Magic Coffee Hair Odds and Ends

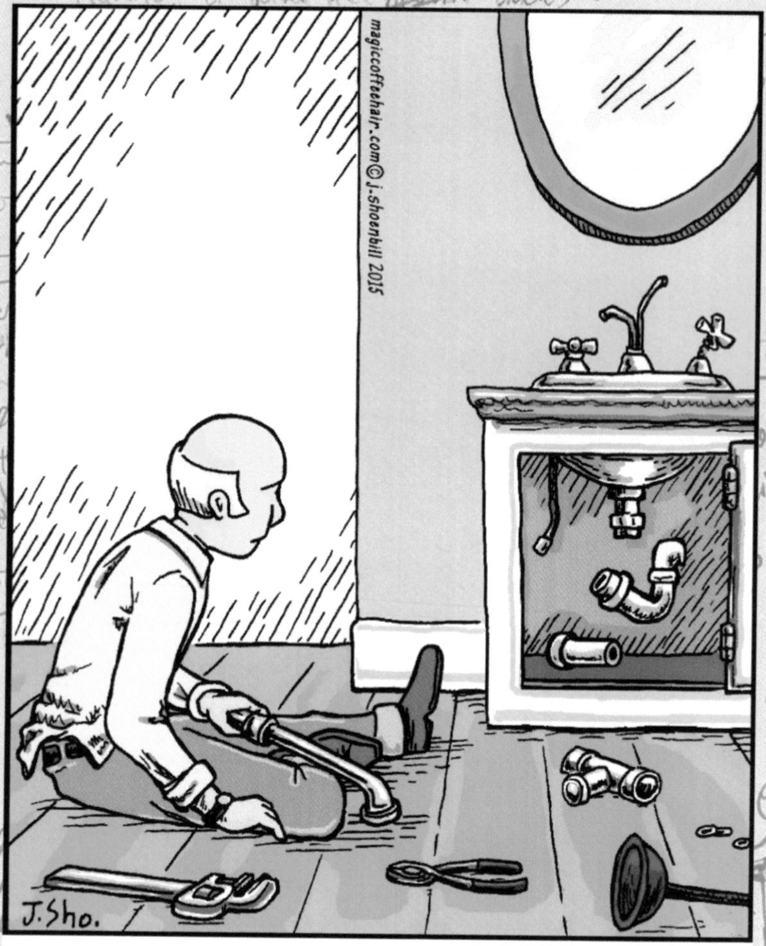

magiccoffeehair.com© j.shoenbill 2015
J.Sho.

From time to time, Carl struggled with plumber's block.

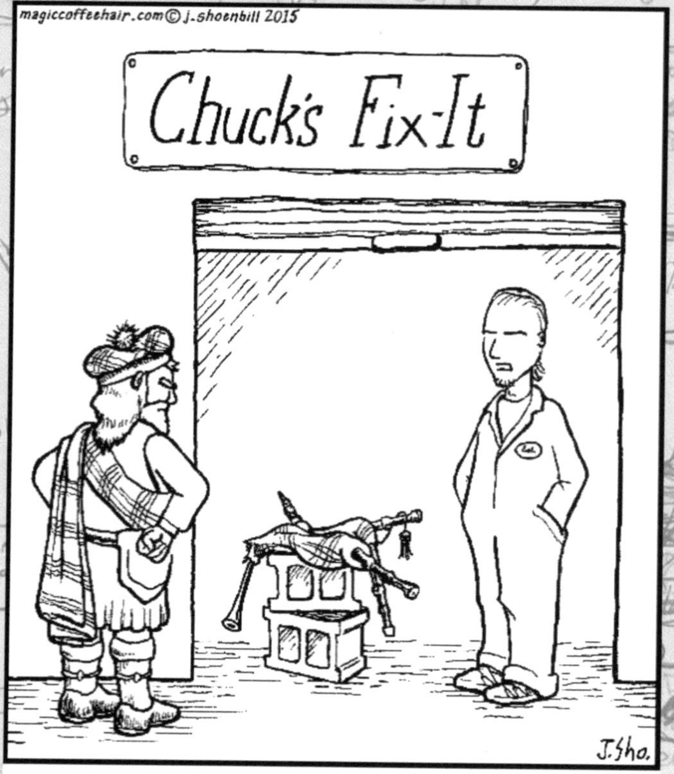

magiccoffeehair.com© j.shoenbill 2015
Chuck's Fix-It
J.Sho.

"Bad flap-valve leak, tenor drones gunked up..
it'll be a week, <u>If</u> I can get the parts."

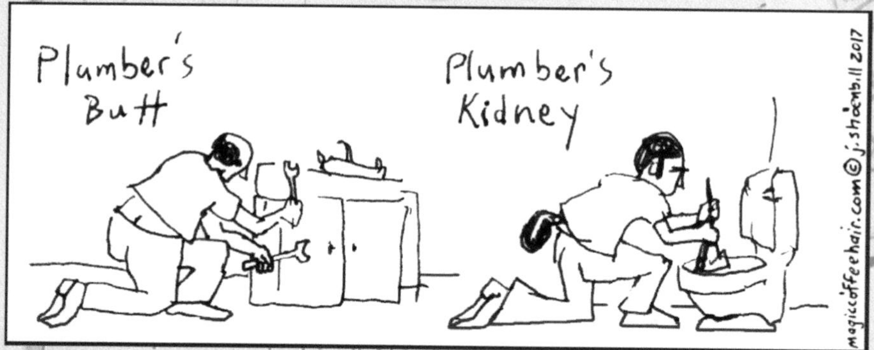

Plumber's Butt
Plumber's Kidney
magiccoffeehair.com© j.shoenbill 2017

Magic Coffee Hair Odds and Ends

Early Futons

"Kids today... only care about latest technology."

GOOD IDEA   BAD IDEA

LITTLE
FREE
LIBRARY

LITTLE
FREE
PHARMACY

Magic Coffee Hair Odds and Ends

"Nice farmer tattoo."

"Are you still working on that?"

Magic Coffee Hair Odds and Ends

FIVE MORE REPS!

The Magic Coffee Hair Fitness System

Bored with their jogging strollers, the very fittest neighborhood moms start up a 'running with furniture' club.

The Magic Coffee Hair Fitness System

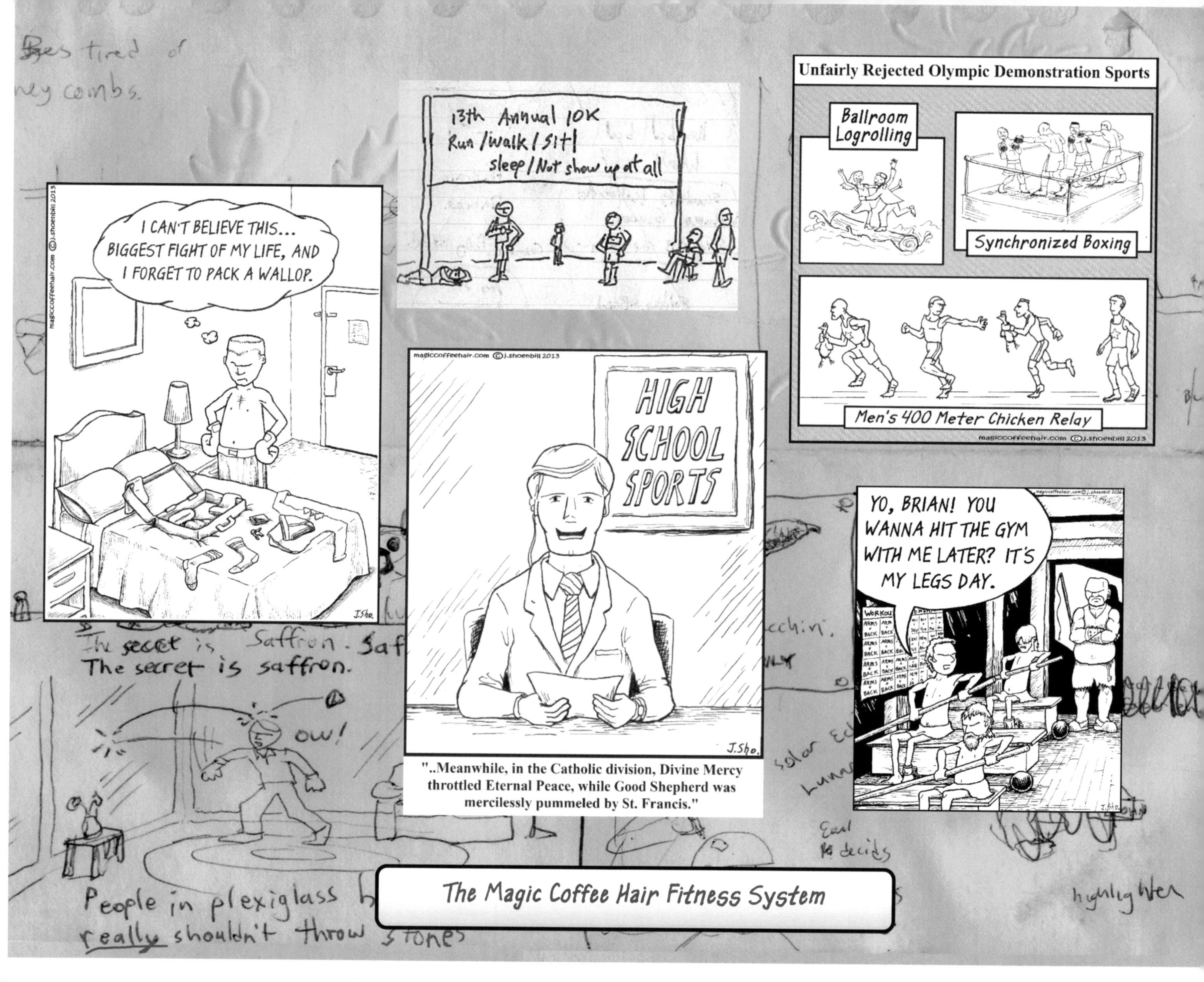
I CAN'T BELIEVE THIS... BIGGEST FIGHT OF MY LIFE, AND I FORGET TO PACK A WALLOP.
magiccoffeehair.com ©j.shoenbill 2013
J.Sho.
13th Annual 10K Run/Walk/Sit/sleep/Not show up at all
Unfairly Rejected Olympic Demonstration Sports
Ballroom Logrolling
Synchronized Boxing
Men's 400 Meter Chicken Relay
magiccoffeehair.com ©j.shoenbill 2013
magiccoffeehair.com ©j.shoenbill 2013
HIGH SCHOOL SPORTS
J.Sho.
"..Meanwhile, in the Catholic division, Divine Mercy throttled Eternal Peace, while Good Shepherd was mercilessly pummeled by St. Francis."
YO, BRIAN! YOU WANNA HIT THE GYM WITH ME LATER? IT'S MY LEGS DAY.
J.Sho.
The secret is saffron.
ow!
The Magic Coffee Hair Fitness System

The guys all hated playing hoops with Greg
on the days he brought "little G" along.

"What do you mean, I wasted my life?
Have you **seen** my abs?"

The Magic Coffee Hair Fitness System

Gym Teacher Job Interview

In a final attempt to get in shape, Gary hires an impersonal trainer.

Yoga Trash Talk

The Magic Coffee Hair Fitness System

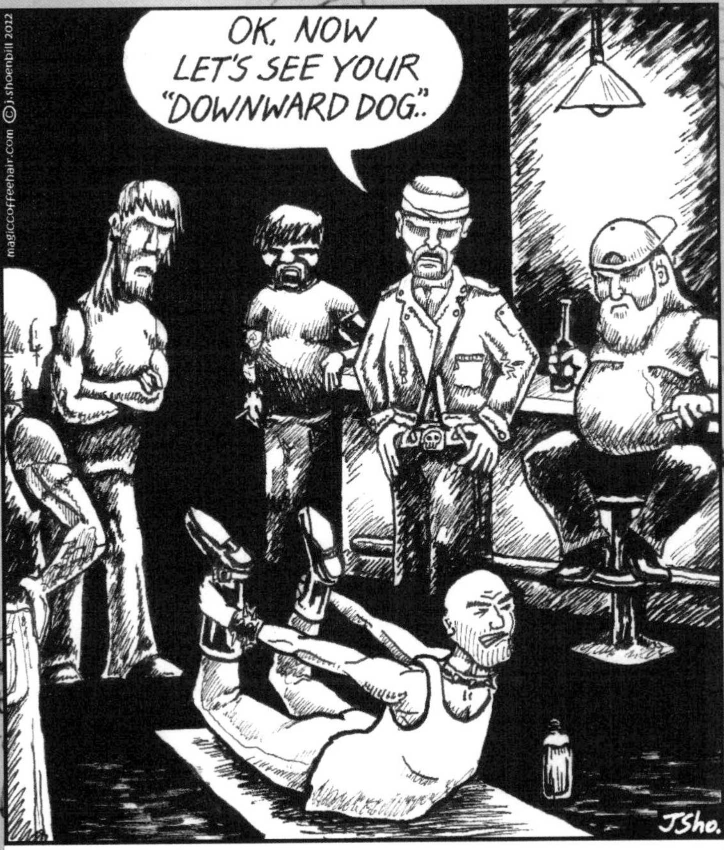
OK, NOW LET'S SEE YOUR "DOWNWARD DOG."
magiccoffeehair.com ©j.shoenbill 2012
JSho.

The Skullsmashers gang were known for their cruel and inhuman initiation rituals.

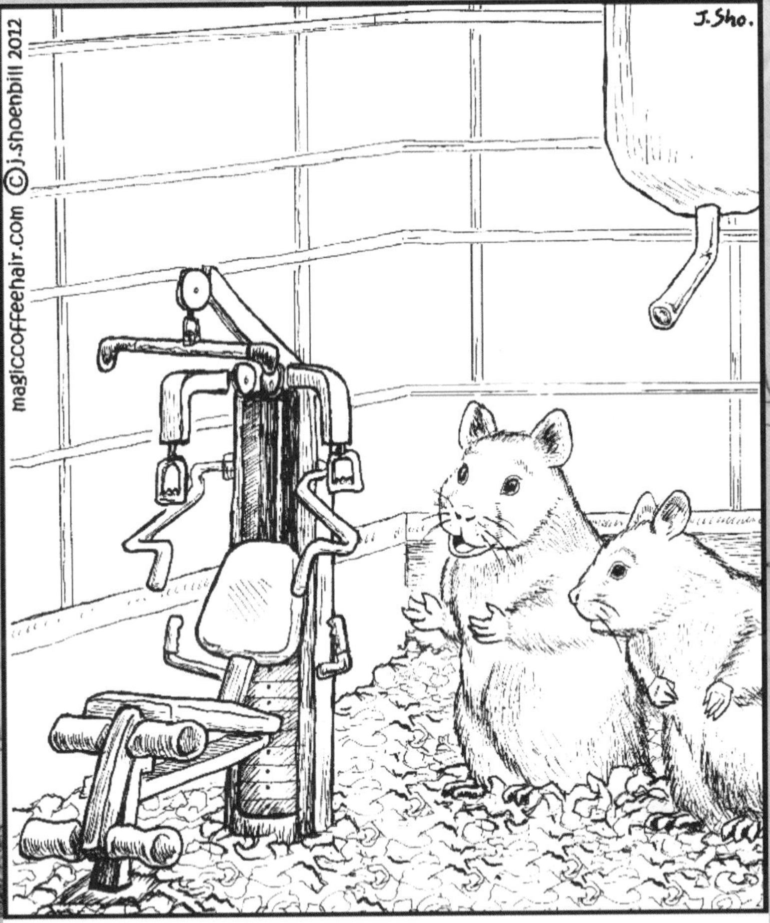
magiccoffeehair.com ©j.shoenbill 2012
J.Sho.

"Yeah, it's nice, but I liked the wheel better."

The Magic Coffee Hair Fitness System

FAQ (Frequently Asked Questions)

No questions are asked of me frequently. But if any were, this is what I might imagine them to be.

Who are you?
My name is Jim, but most people call me Jim. A few call me Jimbob, and to some I'm still Jimmy.

Where did all this come from?
I grew up in a small house surrounded by books, TV, newspapers, magazines, Safari Cards of Knowledge, red shag carpet, and sarcastic older siblings. In school I originally studied art, but was lured away by the siren song of computer science, in which I've had a long career. Magic Coffee Hair was born in 2012 when I drew a cartoon while on standby in the Cleveland Airport, making myself laugh, and worrying other travelers.

Where have you been published?
I'm a regular contributor to Funny Times magazine and have sold and licensed cartoons in a variety of publications, among them a Brazilian high school textbook and an academic treatise on bedbugs.

Can these comics be used, shared, or bought?
They are copyrighted, but please let me know if you have an interest. There are ways.

Who is your favorite literary character?
Max from "Where the Wild Things Are". It was my favorite book as a child, and I haven't read much fiction since then. Close second: The Hardy Boys' stout pal Chet, who regularly falls into holes and gets tied up by bad guys.

Favorite Cartooning Quotes?
"Cartooning is for people who can't quite draw and can't quite write.
You combine the two half-talents and come up with a career." —Matt Groenig
"Master, you delivered to me two talents; here, I have made two talents more." —Matthew 25:22
"I was sixty years old— just a kid with a crazy dream." —Leonard Cohen